W9-CNO-403

MAGNETISM

BY

JOANNA BRUNDLE

Published in 2020 by KidHaven Publishing, an Imprint of Greenhaven Publishing, LLC
353 3rd Avenue, Suite 255, New York, NY 10010

Written by: Joanna Brundle
Edited by: Kirsty Holmes
Designed by: Drue Rintoul

Cataloging-in-Publication Data

Names: Brundle, Joanna.
Title: Magnetism / Joanna Brundle.
Description: New York : KidHaven Publishing, 2020. | Series: Science in action | Includes glossary and index.
Identifiers: ISBN 9781534530898 (pbk.) | ISBN 9781534530188 (library bound) | ISBN 9781534531628 (6 pack) | ISBN 9781534530805 (ebook)
Subjects: LCSH: Magnetism--Juvenile literature. | Magnets--Juvenile literature.
Classification: LCC QC753.7 B786 2020 | DDC 538--dc23

Photo credits
Abbreviations: l-left, r-right, b-bottom, t-top, c-center, m-middle.
Front Cover t – Pichet siritantiwat. Front Cover mt – Pat_Hastings. Front Cover mb –Tyler Olson. Front Cover b – worradirek. 1,2 – Vadim Sadovski. 4tr –
revers. 4b – Silberkorn. 5tr – Aleksandr Pobedimskiy. 5bml – mangax. 5bmr – revers. 5br – NikolayN. 5bl – Fedorov Oleksiy. 6tr – imagedb.com. 6bl
– udaix. 7m – connel. 7b – Africa Studio. 8tr – MrJafari. 8b – haryigit. 9tl – valzan. 9tr – Konjushenko Vladimir. 9m – MilanB. 11t – David M. 12tr – Triff.
12bl – Hayati Kayhan. 13t – DoublePHOTO studio. 13b – Mr. SUTTIPON YAKHAM. 14 – Designua. 15t – Naeblys. 15b – Iordache Gabriel. 16 – Milagli.
17tr – Fotos593. 17b – Bohbeh. 18tr – AngelPet. 18b – BLUR LIFE 1975. 19t – PhotoStock10. 19b – Tyler Olson. 20br – cyo bo. 21t – Zanariah Salam. 21b
– guteksk7. 22t – Designua. 22br – Pair Srinrat. 23tr – yevgeniy11. 23b – Suwin. 24tr – Igor Karasi. 24tl – Bjoern Wylezich. 24br – Grigvovan. 24bl –
PROJEKTNOW. 25tl – MR.PAPASR MAKEE. 25tr – symbiot. 25bl – CHOKCHAI POOMICHAIYA. 25br – Artazum. 26t – Andrey_Popov. 26tl – cowardlion.
26ml – Levent Konuk. 26mr – EcoPrint. 26bl – behindlens. 27tl – ratmaner. 27m – zentilia. 27b – Triff. 28bl – Jay Ondreicka. 28br – Daniel Prudek. 29t
– Willyam Bradberry. 29b – Marco Marchi. 30t – Pincarel. 30m – iurii. 30b – fusebulb.
Images are courtesy of Shutterstock.com. With thanks to Getty Images, Thinkstock Photo and iStockphoto.

Printed in the United States of America

CPSIA compliance information: Batch #BS19KL: For further information contact Greenhaven Publishing LLC, New York, New York at 1-844-317-7404.

CONTENTS

Words that look like **this** are explained in the glossary on page 31.

WHAT IS MAGNETISM?

Magnetism is a force that surrounds us all in our everyday lives. Forces pull and push things. If you have ever played with magnets, you will know that they pull and push one another, and other magnetic objects. Scientists say that magnets attract (pull) and repel (push away).

Magnetism is an unusual force. Most forces work when objects touch one another. Your foot has to make contact with a ball for the ball to move. You need to touch a door in order to push it open or pull it closed. But magnetism works at a distance, without this contact. Try letting go of a fridge magnet just before it touches the door – the magnet jumps onto the door.

As well as working through air and other gases, some magnets are also strong enough to be effective through some solids, for example paper and cardboard. They can also work through liquids, like water, and even through a totally empty space, called a **vacuum**.

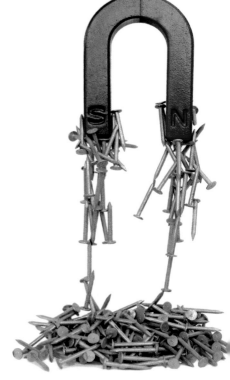

Magnetism is the force that pulls, or attracts, the nails to the magnet, and holds them in place.

The magnetic force of this fridge magnet works through paper to hold the note in place.

WHO DISCOVERED MAGNETISM?

People have known about magnetism for thousands of years. The ancient Greeks discovered an iron-rich **mineral** that could attract other pieces of iron. The mineral, called lodestone, was found in the ground, around 600 BC. The word magnetism comes from the area of Turkey where lodestone was first discovered, called Magnesia.

Lodestone looks like any ordinary rock, but it is a naturally magnetic material.

Ancient Chinese civilizations also discovered **magnetic materials** and put them to good use. The Chinese realized that if a lodestone can swing freely, it always points in the same direction. They used this knowledge to make **magnetic compasses**.

By the 12th century, Chinese sailors were using these compasses to find their way on the high seas. The Chinese also used compasses for fortune-telling and in the art of feng shui – a way of deciding on the luckiest places and ways to build and decorate houses.

Magnets come in all shapes and sizes. Most are made of iron or **compounds**.

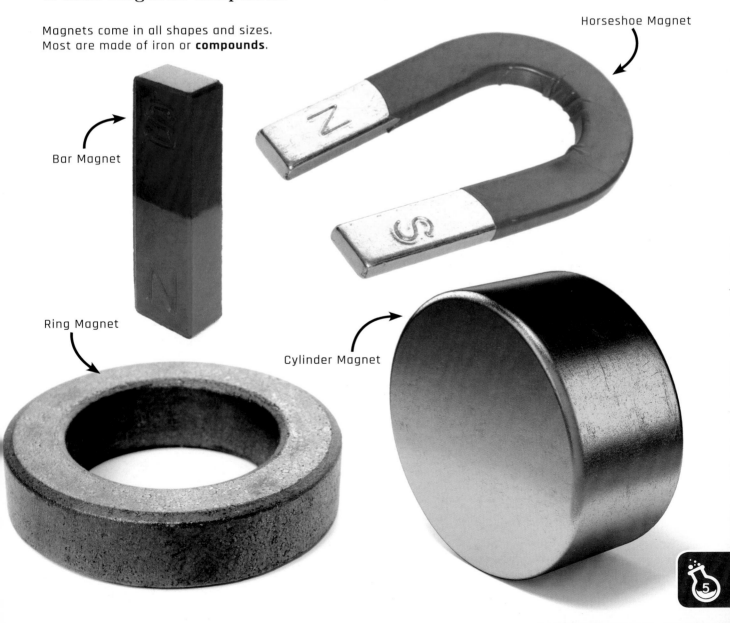

Horseshoe Magnet

Bar Magnet

Ring Magnet

Cylinder Magnet

HOW DO MAGNETS WORK?

Magnets work because they produce an invisible force around themselves called a magnetic force field. A magnet's force field is the area in which the pulling or pushing force of a magnet has an effect. The force is strongest at the ends of the magnet, called the poles. Every magnet has two poles called a north pole and a south pole.

Iron filings scattered around a magnet are attracted to it and settle into a pattern. The pattern shows the extent of the magnet's force field. The lines are called magnetic field lines. The closer they are together, the stronger the magnetic force field.

Opposite, or unlike, poles attract one another, so the north pole of one magnet will attract the south pole of another. The same, or like, poles repel one another, so two north poles or two south poles will push apart.

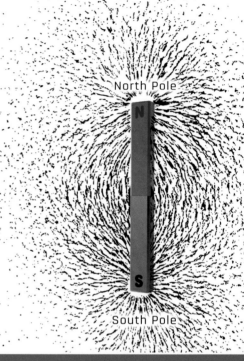

North Pole

South Pole

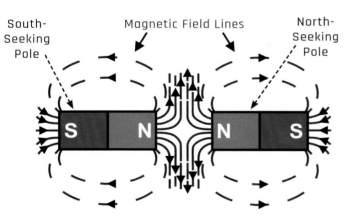

South-Seeking Pole

Magnetic Field Lines

North-Seeking Pole

Two like poles together repel.

Magnetic field lines are closest together at the poles, where a magnet's force field is strongest. The strength of a magnet's force field gradually becomes weaker as the distance from the magnet increases. A magnet held directly over a pile of paper clips picks them up easily, but if you try this with the magnet farther and farther away, the magnet becomes less and less effective.

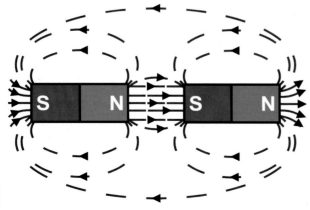

Two unlike poles together attract.

CHARLES COULOMB (1736-1806) WAS A FRENCH PHYSICIST WHO WORKED OUT THAT THE STRENGTH OF A MAGNET'S FORCE FIELD RELATES TO THE DISTANCE BETWEEN THE MAGNET AND THE METAL.

DOMAINS

Magnetic materials contain areas of magnetism called magnetic domains. Domains are made up of clusters of **atoms**. Atoms are the smallest possible particles of a chemical **element**. The atoms act like tiny magnets that are all lined up in the same way, so that each domain becomes a mini magnet with a north and a south pole. If the domains are jumbled up, with their poles pointing in different directions, the mini force fields cancel one another out and the material does not behave as a magnet. If the domains are lined up and all pointing in the same direction, however, the mini force fields work together to create a magnet.

The books in these images represent domains. A magnetic material only behaves like a magnet when all the domains are lined up and facing in the same direction, like the books in this image. Jumbled domains mean a material is not magnetized.

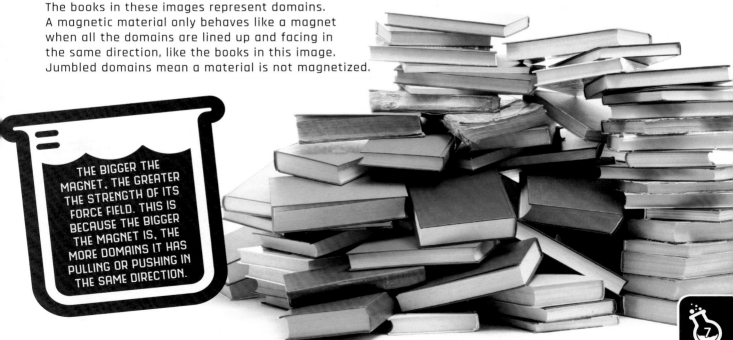

THE BIGGER THE MAGNET, THE GREATER THE STRENGTH OF ITS FORCE FIELD. THIS IS BECAUSE THE BIGGER THE MAGNET IS, THE MORE DOMAINS IT HAS PULLING OR PUSHING IN THE SAME DIRECTION.

CHARGED PARTICLES

Atoms are made up of **neutrons**, **protons**, and **electrons**. Protons and electrons are called charged particles because they carry an electric charge. Electrons carry a negative charge and swirl around the nucleus or central part of the atom. In magnetic elements, it is the special arrangement and movement of these electrons that creates a magnetic force.

Neutrons

Negatively Charged Electrons

Positively Charged Protons

Nucleus

MAGNETISM AND ELECTRICITY

An electric current is a flow of negatively charged electrons. This flow of electricity creates a magnetic field in a cylinder shape around the path of the current. A temporary but powerful type of magnet, called an electromagnet, can be made by passing an electric current through a wire coiled around a piece of metal containing a magnetic metal called iron. The magnetic field set up by the flow of electricity then magnetizes the piece of metal.

MAKE A FIST WITH YOUR THUMB STICKING OUT. YOUR THUMB REPRESENTS THE DIRECTION OF THE FLOW OF AN ELECTRIC CURRENT THROUGH A WIRE. YOUR FINGERS REPRESENT THE MAGNETIC FIELD CREATED AROUND THE WIRE.

Battery (Power Supply)

Paper Clips

A Simple Electromagnet

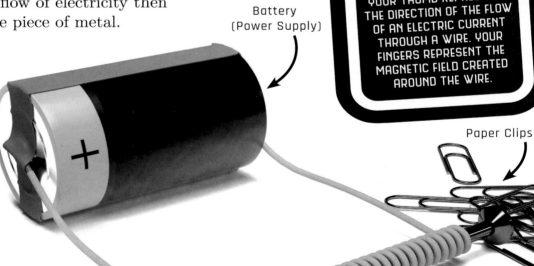

Metal Rod (Containing Iron)

The paper clips are attracted by the metal rod, which becomes a temporary electromagnet when electricity passes through the wire.

MAKING MAGNETS

Although iron is magnetic, some objects that contain iron are not. How can this be? Well, we know that things aren't magnetic if the domains are jumbled up. So, if the domains could be made to line up, could we turn an ordinary piece of metal into a magnet? Try this simple experiment to find out.

YOU WILL NEED

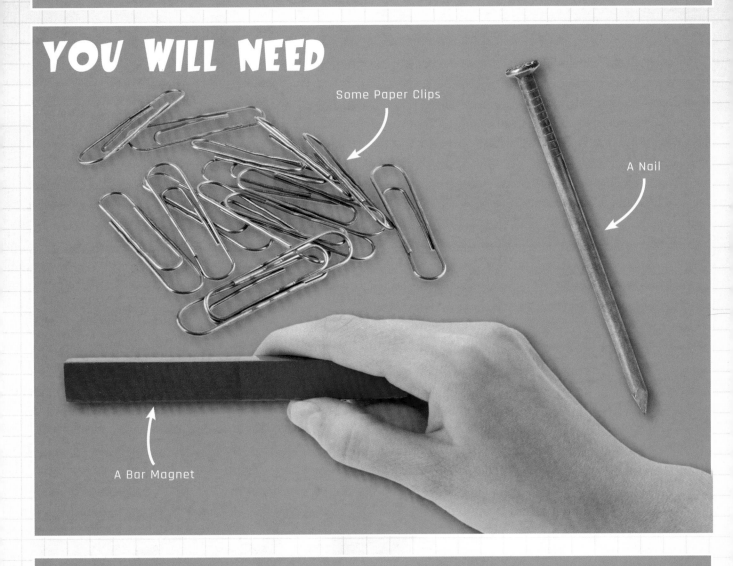

Some Paper Clips

A Nail

A Bar Magnet

MAKE YOUR MAGNET

Check that the nail is not magnetized by holding it over the paper clips. If it's not magnetized, it won't pick any of them up. Next, carefully stroke the magnet over the nail ten times. Lift the magnet at the end of each stroke and always stroke in the same direction. Then see how many paper clips the nail can pick up. Now stroke the magnet over the nail 20 times and see if there is a difference. Check how long the magnetism lasts and carefully record that, too.

CHECK YOUR RESULTS

You should find that stroking the magnet over the nail turns it into a temporary magnet. The more you stroke, the stronger the magnet becomes and the longer the magnetism lasts.

PRESERVING AND DESTROYING MAGNETS

As our experiment shows, temporary magnets quickly lose their magnetism. An electromagnet only works while an electric current is flowing. But it is very difficult to destroy a permanent magnet. The process of turning a magnet into a nonmagnet is called demagnetization.

You can demagnetize a magnet by dropping it or by hitting it with a hammer. This causes the magnetic domains to move so that they are no longer lined up. Heating a magnetic metal beyond a certain temperature, called the Curie Point, also destroys its magnetic properties. The Curie Point for iron is 1,418°F (770°C).

IF YOU CUT A PERMANENT MAGNET IN HALF, EACH HALF BECOMES A NEW MAGNET. ALTHOUGH THE NEW MAGNETS WILL BE WEAKER BECAUSE THEY ARE SMALLER, EACH WILL STILL HAVE ITS OWN NORTH AND SOUTH POLE.

The Curie Point is named after the French scientist Pierre Curie, who discovered that magnetic materials lose their magnetic properties when heated above a certain temperature.

SOME VERY LARGE, POWERFUL MAGNETS ARE PRESERVED BY KEEPING THEM IN EXTREMELY COLD CONDITIONS. THE COLD STOPS THE DOMAINS FROM MOVING AND ENSURES THAT THEY STAY LINED UP. MAGNETIC STRENGTH ACTUALLY INCREASES AT LOWER TEMPERATURES.

So we know that magnetic fields are effective through gases, solids, liquids, and vacuums. Some materials, however, can be used to contain or block a magnetic field. This process is called magnetic shielding. It is used in pieces of equipment that need to use magnets in a very careful, controlled way, such as the MRI scanner that we'll look at on page 19. Many electromagnetic objects, such as a computer's main storage device (called a hard drive), can be damaged by magnetic fields. A magnetic shielding material called mu-metal can be used to contain a magnetic field and stop this kind of damage. Mu-metal contains iron, **nickel**, and other metals.

Electrical transformers are used in **power stations** to change the power of an electric current. They are often coated in mu-metal. This stops their magnetic field from damaging nearby equipment.

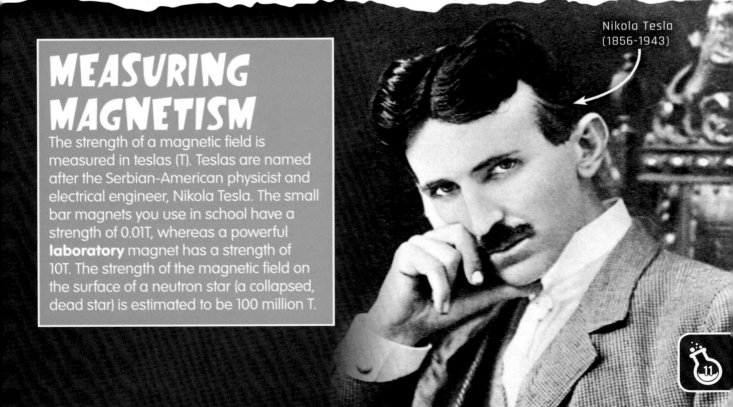

Nikola Tesla (1856-1943)

MEASURING MAGNETISM

The strength of a magnetic field is measured in teslas (T). Teslas are named after the Serbian-American physicist and electrical engineer, Nikola Tesla. The small bar magnets you use in school have a strength of 0.01T, whereas a powerful **laboratory** magnet has a strength of 10T. The strength of the magnetic field on the surface of a neutron star (a collapsed, dead star) is estimated to be 100 million T.

MAGNETIC MATERIALS

Magnetic materials are materials that are attracted to a magnet or that can be magnetized.

MAGNETIC ELEMENTS

The most common magnetic material is iron, a metallic element that makes up around 5 percent of the **Earth's crust**. Nickel and **cobalt** are also magnetic metals. The periodic table is a chart that chemists use to list and describe all the known elements. Elements that belong to a part of the periodic table called rare Earth metals also make good magnets, like neodymium. This magnetic material is found in many everyday items including headphones and computer hard drives. All these elements are known as ferromagnetic materials.

Mars Exploration Rover (MER)

Neodymium magnets are used on MER vehicles exploring the planet Mars. The magnets collect dust from Mars for examination and testing.

These are some nonmagnetic materials.

MAGNETIC ELEMENTS

Most other common metals, such as copper, gold, silver, and **aluminum**, are not magnetic. Common nonmetallic materials such as wood, paper, glass, plastics, and food items are not magnetic, either.

Most drink cans are made of aluminum, which is a nonmagnetic material.

ALLOYS

Some of the best magnetic materials are alloys. An alloy is a mixture of a metallic element and different metal or nonmetallic element that creates a new material. Steel is a common alloy, made by mixing iron and carbon. There are many different types of steel, but most are magnetic because they contain so much iron.

NONMAGNETIC AND MAGNETIC COMPOUNDS

Compounds are substances that are formed when two or more elements are chemically joined – or bonded – together. Although iron is magnetic, some compounds of iron are not. When iron reacts chemically with **oxygen**, it creates an orangey-red powder called iron oxide or rust. This powder is a compound of iron and oxygen. It is not magnetic because iron atoms lose their magnetism as they react with oxygen.

Like rust, lodestone is a compound of iron and oxygen. Unlike rust, however, lodestone is magnetic because of its crystal-like structure. Crystals are solids in which the atoms are arranged in an ordered way. In lodestone, the iron atoms are lined up in this ordered pattern.

The iron oxide on this old boat is not magnetic, because iron atoms lose their magnetism as they rust.

MAGNETICALLY HARD AND SOFT MATERIALS

Some materials, like the nail in our experiment on page 9, can be made into good temporary magnets that lose their magnetism when they are removed from a magnetic field. These materials are said to be magnetically soft. Materials that keep their magnetism even when they are removed from a magnetic field make good permanent magnets. These materials are said to be magnetically hard.

13

MAGNETIC EARTH

*The Earth's core, or center, has two layers: an inner and an outer core. The inner core is a solid ball of iron, almost the size of the moon, while the outer core is a thick layer of **molten** nickel and iron. As we know, both nickel and iron are magnetic, so the Earth itself is a giant magnet. Just as electrons swirl around the nucleus of an atom, the molten outer core of the Earth rotates around the solid inner core. This sets up a giant magnetic field around the Earth.*

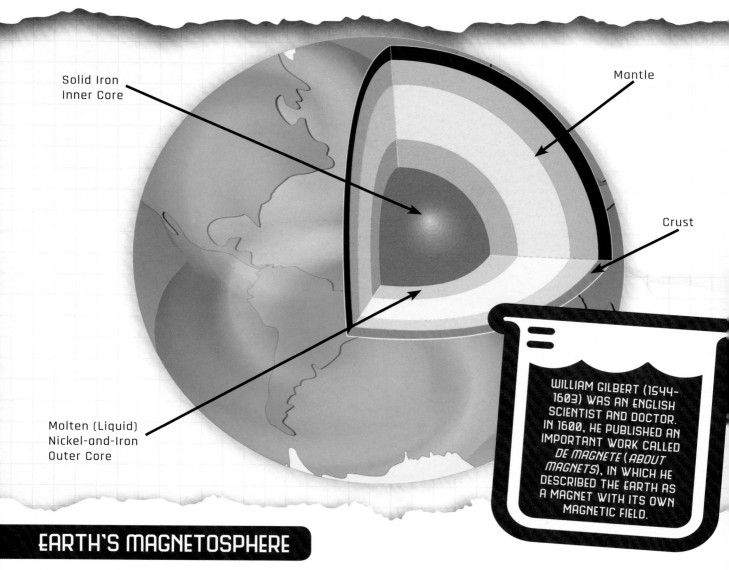

Solid Iron
Inner Core

Mantle

Crust

Molten (Liquid)
Nickel-and-Iron
Outer Core

WILLIAM GILBERT (1544-1603) WAS AN ENGLISH SCIENTIST AND DOCTOR. IN 1600, HE PUBLISHED AN IMPORTANT WORK CALLED *DE MAGNETE* (*ABOUT MAGNETS*), IN WHICH HE DESCRIBED THE EARTH AS A MAGNET WITH ITS OWN MAGNETIC FIELD.

EARTH'S MAGNETOSPHERE

The Earth's magnetic field stretches thousands of miles into space. This area around the Earth in which its magnetic force is effective is called its magnetosphere. The planets Jupiter, Saturn, Uranus, and Venus all have magnetic fields that are much more powerful than Earth's. Jupiter's magnetic field is the most powerful.

EFFECTS OF THE MAGNETOSPHERE

The sun is an intensely hot ball of burning gases. Heat and light from the sun are very important for life on Earth, but the sun also sends out solar wind that carries huge quantities of electrically charged particles. Solar wind streams off the sun in all directions at speeds of up to 248.5 miles (400 km) per second. If all the particles carried by solar wind reached the Earth's surface, it would cause a lot of damage. Fortunately, the Earth's magnetic field acts like a giant umbrella, shielding us from these harmful particles.

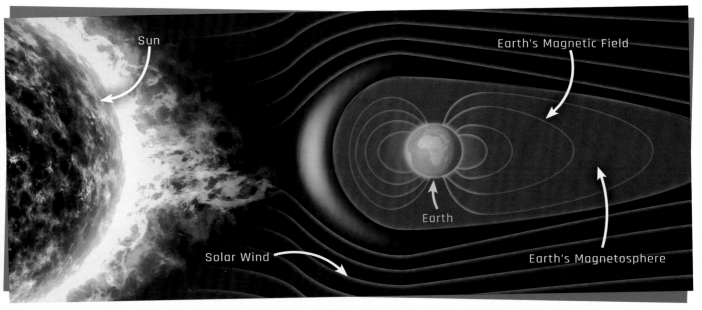

The diagram shows how the Earth's magnetic field deflects or bends the stream of solar wind away from the surface of the Earth.

AURORAS

Sometimes, the magnetosphere is responsible for light shows in the sky called auroras. Auroras happen when particles from solar wind that manage to enter the magnetosphere are drawn towards the magnetic poles and collide with oxygen and **nitrogen** in the Earth's atmosphere. This produces spectacular waving ribbons of colored light. Oxygen creates green auroras whereas nitrogen creates blue and reddish-purple auroras. Auroras are usually seen near the Earth's magnetic poles, where the magnetic field is at its strongest, but some have been spotted as far south as California.

Auroras are called the northern lights (or Aurora Borealis) near the North Pole and the southern lights (or Aurora Australis) near the South Pole.

THE EARTH'S POLES

The Earth's geographic poles are the North Pole and the South Pole. These are found at the ends of the **Earth's axis**. The Earth spins or rotates around this axis. But the Earth also has magnetic poles, like any other magnet. These magnetic poles are close to the geographic poles but are not in exactly the same place. The exact position of the magnetic poles actually changes slightly all the time, because the swirling currents of molten metal in the core affect the Earth's magnetic field. It is because the Earth's magnetic poles are found near the geographic North and South Poles that the poles of magnets were given their name.

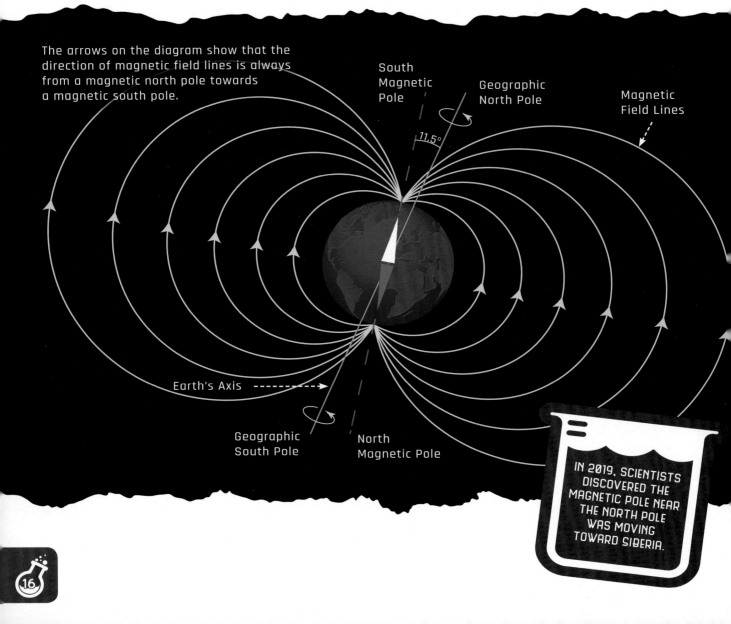

The arrows on the diagram show that the direction of magnetic field lines is always from a magnetic north pole towards a magnetic south pole.

South Magnetic Pole

Geographic North Pole

Magnetic Field Lines

11.5°

Earth's Axis

Geographic South Pole

North Magnetic Pole

IN 2019, SCIENTISTS DISCOVERED THE MAGNETIC POLE NEAR THE NORTH POLE WAS MOVING TOWARD SIBERIA.

SURPRISING POLES

If you look closely at the diagram on page 16, you will see something rather surprising. The North Magnetic Pole is actually near the geographic South Pole, and the South Magnetic Pole is near the geographic North Pole. It all sounds rather confusing, but if you remember that Earth is one big magnet and that opposite poles attract, it is easier to understand. The needle in a compass is a tiny bar magnet that spins freely and always lines itself up with the Earth's magnetic field. Wherever the north pole of the compass magnet points or is attracted to must actually be the Magnetic South Pole.

Walkers use a compass and map to find their way. The compass needle actually points to the Magnetic South Pole, but as this is so close to the geographic North Pole, it makes no difference to the direction taken.

FLIPPING POLES

Scientists who study rock samples know that the Earth's magnetic field flips or reverses from time to time. The magnetic north and south poles change places roughly every 500,000 years. Scientists have found rocks on the ocean floor that contain iron atoms lined up with the Earth's magnetic field. Molten lava from erupting volcanoes cooled to form these rocks. As the lava solidified, the iron atoms it contained lined up with the Earth's magnetic field. But different bands of rock of different ages are lined up differently, with some pointing south and some pointing north. This discovery proves that Earth's magnetic poles have reversed themselves many times. No one knows why this happens!

ELECTROMAGNETS

Electromagnets can be very simple (like the one seen on page 8), or they can be powerful enough to lift heavy materials.

HOW DO ELECTROMAGNETS WORK?

An electric current flowing through a wire sets up a weak magnetic field around the wire. The magnetic field can be made much stronger by winding the wire into a coil called a **solenoid**. If the coil or solenoid is placed around a piece of iron, the magnetic field becomes even stronger. The magnet created is called an electromagnet. Like permanent magnets, electromagnets have two poles and they attract only iron and the other magnetic metals we looked at on page 12.

This electromagnet is being used in a scrapyard to separate magnetic metals from nonmagnetic materials. The magnetic materials are attracted to the magnet and are held in place by the attracting force of opposite poles.

CHANGING THE POWER OF AN ELECTROMAGNET

An important advantage of an electromagnet is that it is possible to control its power. The strength of an electromagnet depends on the strength of the electric current that is passed through the wire and the number of times that the wire is coiled. By increasing either or both of these things, it is possible to create a more powerful magnet.

THE NATIONAL HIGH MAGNETIC FIELD LABORATORY (MAGNET LAB) IN FLORIDA IS HOME TO SOME OF THE WORLD'S LARGEST AND MOST POWERFUL ELECTROMAGNETS. RESEARCH AT THIS LABORATORY IS HELPING TO IMPROVE OUR UNDERSTANDING OF MANY AREAS OF LIFE, INCLUDING MATERIALS, ENERGY, AND HEALTH.

USING ELECTROMAGNETS

Permanent magnets, such as fridge magnets, stay magnetic all the time. Electromagnets, however, can be turned on and off, because they only work when the electric current is switched on. This makes electromagnets extremely useful. We can use them, for example, to lift heavy materials into position and then drop them exactly where they are needed when the current is switched off. Electromagnets are used on building and construction sites to lift steel into position.

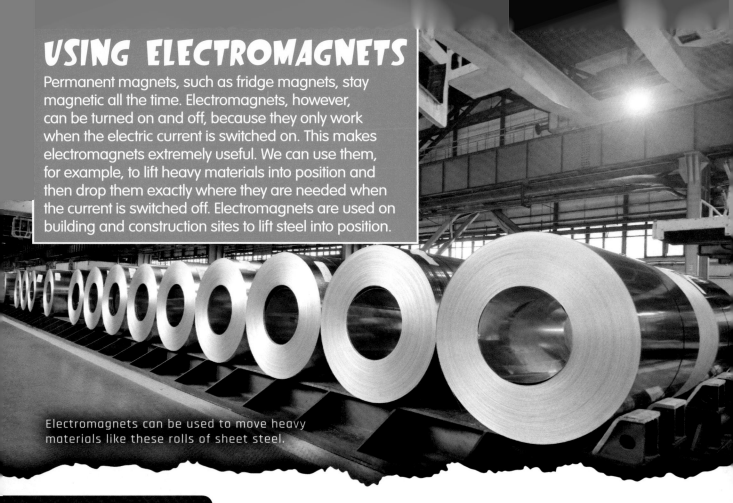

Electromagnets can be used to move heavy materials like these rolls of sheet steel.

MRI SCANNERS

One of the most important uses of electromagnets is in Magnetic Resonance Imaging (MRI) scanners, which allow doctors to see inside patients' bodies. When an electric current passes through wire coils in the scanner, a powerful electromagnet is created and **radio waves** are sent into the body. Our bodies are mostly made up of water, which contains hydrogen and oxygen atoms. The radio waves cause protons in the hydrogen atoms in the body to move and send back a radio signal. Signals from millions of protons combine to make a picture of the part of the body being scanned.

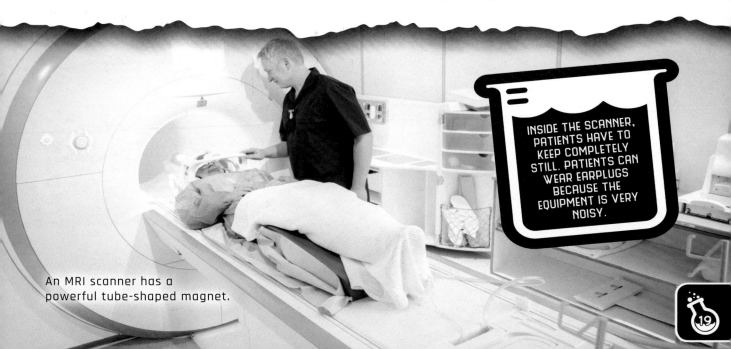

An MRI scanner has a powerful tube-shaped magnet.

INSIDE THE SCANNER, PATIENTS HAVE TO KEEP COMPLETELY STILL. PATIENTS CAN WEAR EARPLUGS BECAUSE THE EQUIPMENT IS VERY NOISY.

MAGNETS AND MOTION

UNDERSTANDING FRICTION

If you stop pedaling your bicycle, you will gradually slow down without having to brake. This is because a force called friction is at work. Friction happens when things rub against each other, like your bike tires and the road. Friction pushes against the direction in which something is trying to move. Engineers try to reduce friction when they want to make a vehicle, like a car or train, travel as fast as possible.

MAGLEV TRAINS

Maglev trains have no wheels. They use magnets to raise them above the track, so the force of friction is removed. Magnets on the tracks and on the undersides of these trains are arranged so that the like poles repel, pushing the train upward, away from the track. The track in front of the train also carries magnets which attract, pulling the train forward. Magnets on the track behind the train repel, pushing it forward. The magnets used are powerful electromagnets that can be switched on and off to move the train quickly and then stop it safely at the end of its high-speed journey.

ALTHOUGH THEY ARE ENERGY EFFICIENT AND MAKE LITTLE NOISE OR **POLLUTION**, MAGLEV TRAINS AND TRACKS ARE VERY EXPENSIVE TO BUILD.

MAGLEV IS SHORT FOR MAGNETIC LEVITATION. LEVITATION MEANS RISING UP INTO THE AIR, WITHOUT ANY SUPPORT.

Removing the slowing force of friction allows maglev trains to travel incredibly quickly. During testing in Japan in 2015, a maglev train reached 374.7 miles (603 km) per hour!

ROLLER COASTERS

Electromagnets are used in many amusement park rides, including roller coasters. When the ride starts, electromagnets on the car move closer to other electromagnets on the track. Switching on the electric current activates the magnets. At first, opposite poles attract, pulling the cars onto the tracks, but the current is then quickly reversed. Like poles then repel one another, pushing the cars forward at great speed. This process is called magnetic propulsion.

Roller coasters that use magnetic propulsion can accelerate very quickly, giving a thrilling ride.

THE FLIGHT OF FEAR ROLLER COASTER IN THE U.S. WAS THE FIRST TO USE MAGNETIC PROPULSION. IT OPENED IN 1996.

Electromagnets are also used as brakes for roller coasters. Opposite poles on the cars and on the tracks attract, pulling the car and track together. This slows the roller coaster, smoothly and safely. The power of the electromagnets is gradually increased so that, when the roller coaster reaches the last set of magnets, it stops completely. Electromagnetic roller coasters are safer than old-fashioned rides. The magnets are controlled by fully automated systems, so there is no chance of humans making a mistake. The magnets also keep the cars fully in contact with the track all the way through the ride.

THE ELECTRIC MOTORS THAT POWER ELECTRIC VEHICLES LIKE THIS REQUIRE MAGNETS TO WORK. KEEP READING TO FIND OUT HOW ELECTRIC MOTORS WORK.

MOTORS
AND GENERATORS

ELECTRIC MOTORS

Electric motors change electrical energy into movement energy. They do this using two magnets: a permanent magnet and a temporary electromagnet. As we have already seen, when an electric current is passed through a wire, it creates a magnetic field around the wire. In an electric motor, the electromagnet is positioned inside the magnetic field of the permanent magnet. When the electric current is turned on, the magnetic field of the electromagnet pushes and pulls the magnetic field of the permanent magnet. This causes the electromagnet to spin. This spinning movement is then used to turn an **axle**, which in turn makes other parts of a machine move.

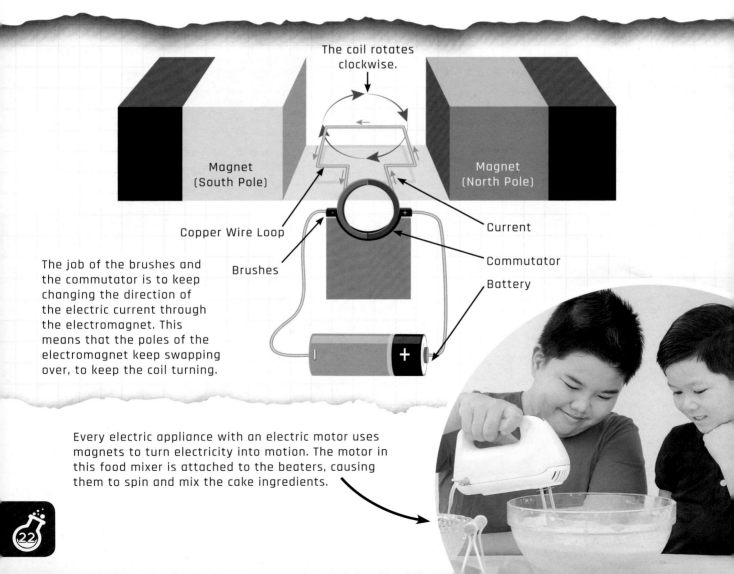

The coil rotates clockwise.

Magnet (South Pole)

Magnet (North Pole)

Copper Wire Loop

Current

Brushes

Commutator

Battery

The job of the brushes and the commutator is to keep changing the direction of the electric current through the electromagnet. This means that the poles of the electromagnet keep swapping over, to keep the coil turning.

Every electric appliance with an electric motor uses magnets to turn electricity into motion. The motor in this food mixer is attached to the beaters, causing them to spin and mix the cake ingredients.

GENERATORS

Just as electricity can produce magnetism, magnets can be used to make electricity. An electric current will flow in a moving wire placed within the magnetic field of a magnet. Moving the magnet also makes an electric current flow through the wire. You can increase the strength of the current by using lots of coils in the wire or by using a stronger magnet. Simple generators use a power source, such as a gas engine, to turn a wire loop between the poles of a magnet. This sets up a flow of electric current through the wire. The wire loop is connected to an electric circuit so that the electricity produced by the generator can be used to power equipment.

Small portable generators are useful for camping trips or outdoor events where there is no main electricity supply. They have power outlets into which campers can plug electrical appliances or tools.

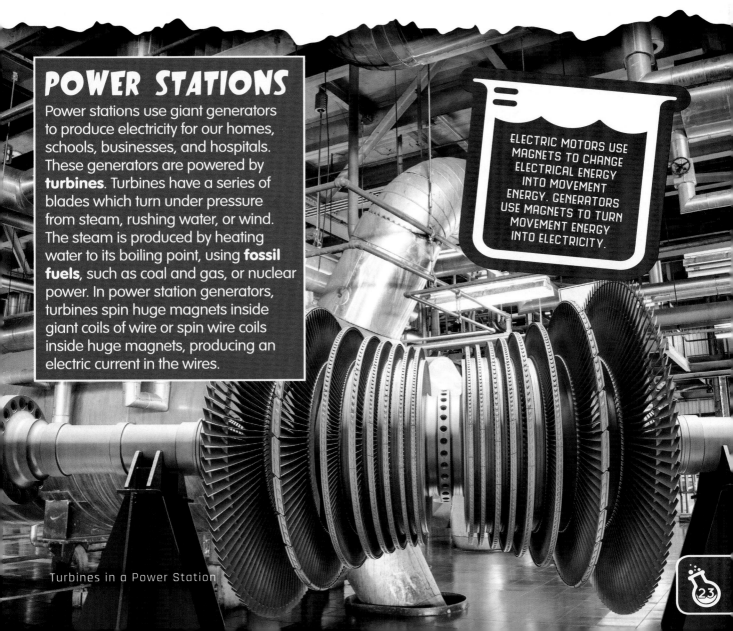

POWER STATIONS

Power stations use giant generators to produce electricity for our homes, schools, businesses, and hospitals. These generators are powered by **turbines**. Turbines have a series of blades which turn under pressure from steam, rushing water, or wind. The steam is produced by heating water to its boiling point, using **fossil fuels**, such as coal and gas, or nuclear power. In power station generators, turbines spin huge magnets inside giant coils of wire or spin wire coils inside huge magnets, producing an electric current in the wires.

ELECTRIC MOTORS USE MAGNETS TO CHANGE ELECTRICAL ENERGY INTO MOVEMENT ENERGY. GENERATORS USE MAGNETS TO TURN MOVEMENT ENERGY INTO ELECTRICITY.

Turbines in a Power Station

HOW DO WE USE MAGNETS ?

Electromagnets are used in the metal detectors found in airports and prisons. These scanners are used to detect weapons. When electricity flows through wire coils in the scanner, it sets up a magnetic field. This magnetic field sweeps through any metal object in the scanner and creates an electric current inside it. This flowing electric current creates another magnetic field around the metal object. The scanner detects this field and sounds an alarm. Metal detecting is also a popular hobby. People use handheld scanners to find buried treasures. In 2012, 50,000 silver coins were found in Europe's Channel Islands. The treasure had been hidden from Roman invaders around 25 BC.

Magnets hold purses and bags safely closed, so that nothing falls out and no one can steal personal items like money or cell phones.

Carpenters use magnetic belts and wristbands to hold screws in a handy position until they are ready to use them.

24

Magnets can be fitted on the underside of street cleaning trucks to pick up magnetic trash that may have been left in the street.

Cows and other farm animals, like goats, sometimes eat metal by accident, especially on farms that are open to the public. Vets can insert magnets into the stomachs of these animals to remove metal objects that could cause serious harm to the animals.

Magnets are very useful in recycling plants. Food cans are highly magnetic, whereas aluminum drink cans are not. Magnets can be used to split them up so that they can be recycled separately.

Washing machines, dryers, dishwashers, hair dryers, and anything with an electric motor all use permanent magnets and temporary electromagnets.

Vending machines, parking meters, and hot drink machines use magnets to sort genuine coins from fakes. Paper money has magnetic dust in its ink to help prevent people from making counterfeit, or fake, bills. Sensors in the machines can detect and reject fake bills.

Ores are natural, solid materials such as rocks that contain valuable minerals or metals. Scientists working with mining companies use sensitive magnetic equipment to study the force lines of the Earth's magnetic field. Distortions, or bends, in the field lines can mean that rocks containing iron are below the surface. Mining companies remove and sell the valuable ore from which the iron is extracted.

Iron Ore Mine

Iron Ore

Gas and Oil Refinery

Bearings are devices used in machinery. They enable machinery to move at very high speeds by reducing friction between moving parts. Some bearings use metal balls or oil to reduce friction. Magnetic bearings remove the force of friction completely, thanks to magnetic levitation (see page 24). They use the repelling force of like poles to keep parts of the bearing separated from one another. Magnetic bearings are used in power stations and in plants that handle natural gas and oil.

Card Reader

Magnetic Strip

There are magnetic strips on the back of bank cards and cards used to enter hotel rooms, apartment buildings, or any other area where only certain people are allowed. The strip uses patterns of magnetism to store information about the cardholder and the card. The information can be read by a magnetic card reader.

The hard drive of a computer is the place where information is stored. Electromagnets write and read data on a computer's hard drive. Hard drives are coated in a magnetic material. Tiny sections of this coating are magnetized by the magnetic field set up by an electromagnet. When you want to look at the information, another electromagnet changes the magnetic information back into electrical signals that are seen on your computer screen.

Computer Hard Drives

While exploring Mars, robotic spacecraft used magnets to attract dust from the atmosphere. Magnetic material in the dust, like iron particles, was picked up by the magnets. This helped the scientists understand what the dust on Mars was made of.

ANIMAL MAGNETISM

Some animals are able to use the Earth's magnetic field to help them navigate, or find their way around. Homing pigeons, for example, can find their way home, even when they are released many miles away, using their ability to sense the strength and angle of the Earth's magnetic field. They are able to do this thanks to small particles of magnetic material in their brains. Many creatures such as bats, salmon, and fruit flies are also known to have this ability, known as magnetoreception.

Homing pigeons were used to carry messages during World War I and World War II because of their ability to navigate. Some were awarded medals for bravery, including Cher Ami, who flew 12 missions and saved the lives of many soldiers, despite being injured herself.

HANS FROMME

The fact that some animals can pick up on Earth's magnetic field was noticed by chance in the autumn of 1957. A scientist at Frankfurt Zoo, Hans Fromme, saw that European robins kept fluttering towards the southwest corner of their cage. Robins migrate from Germany in a southwesterly direction to spend the winter in Spain. The strange thing was that the robins were kept in a shuttered room, but still knew when and in which direction to migrate. Fromme concluded they must be using the Earth's invisible magnetic field.

Brown bats and bees are also known to use the Earth's magnetic field to find their way.

TURTLES

Sea turtles, such as the loggerhead turtle, are perhaps the best navigators of all. Once they hatch from eggs laid in the sand, the baby turtles, called hatchlings, begin a long migration. After swimming thousands of miles, they are able to return to the exact stretch of beach on which they were born. Turtles need special conditions, including soft sand and a quiet beach, to breed successfully.

Loggerhead Turtle

GEOMAGNETIC IMPRINTING IS THE SCIENTIFIC TERM USED FOR THE TURTLE'S ABILITY TO FIND ITS WAY.

Turtles hatch from eggs laid in the sand.

Turtles seem to know that conditions were right on the beach where they were born, and so they return to the same beach to have their own young. Turtles are able to imprint, or learn, the unique magnetic field patterns for their stretch of coastline. They use these patterns to guide them out at sea and to steer them toward the nesting sites chosen by their mothers.

NEW USES FOR MAGNETISM

Some sports can cause serious head injuries if players crash into one another. Magnetized helmets are being developed which could reduce the danger. Remember that like poles repel one another. Magnets fitted on the front and sides of these helmets could be arranged so that the helmets would slightly repel one another. This would lessen the force of a collision and help to prevent **concussion**.

In the near future, magnets will be used to create elevators that don't need cables. These future elevators will be able to go side to side as well as up and down.

Scientists are developing ways of using magnets to fight a serious disease called cancer. One idea is a pill that contains tiny particles of a harmless magnetic material. These particles would attach themselves to cancer cells in a patient's blood. The magnetized particles would then gather on a sensor, worn on the wrist. By looking at information from the sensor, doctors would be able to detect cancers very early, giving patients a better chance of recovery.

GLOSSARY

aluminum	a silvery-gray metallic element that is not magnetic
atoms	the smallest possible particles of a chemical element, made up of a central nucleus surrounded by moving electrons
axle	a rod, either fixed or spinning, that transfers movement to a different part of a machine
cobalt	a silvery-white metallic element that is magnetic
compounds	substances formed from two or more elements, bonded or joined together in a chemical reaction
concussion	a temporary loss of consciousness or a feeling of being dazed and confused, following a blow to the head
Earth's axis	an imaginary line through the center of the Earth from pole to pole, around which the Earth rotates or spins
Earth's crust	the rocky outer layer of the Earth
electrons	tiny, negatively charged particles of an atom that move around the nucleus
elements	substances that cannot be broken down into simpler substances and contain only one type of atom
fossil fuels	fuels such as coal, oil, and gas that formed millions of years ago from the remains of animals and plants
iron filings	small pieces of scrap iron
laboratory	a room or building used for scientific experiments and research
magnetic compasses	instruments used for navigation with a freely swinging, magnetized needle that lines itself up with the Earth's magnetic poles
magnetic materials	substances that are attracted to a magnet or that can be magnetized
mineral	a natural, useful, and sometimes valuable substance, often obtained from rocks in the ground
molten	turned into a liquid by heating
neutrons	tiny particles that carry no charge, found in the nucleus of an atom
nickel	a silvery-white metallic, magnetic element that is commonly used in alloys
nitrogen	a colorless gas that forms around 78 percent of the Earth's atmosphere
oxygen	a colorless gas that forms around 20 percent of the Earth's atmosphere
pollution	harmful or poisonous substances introduced into the environment by the actions of humans
power stations	places where electricity is generated on an industrial scale
protons	tiny positively charged particles, found in the nucleus of an atom
radio waves	invisible electromagnetic waves that travel through the air, vacuums, or other substances
solenoid	a cylinder-shaped coil of wire that acts as a magnet when carrying electric current
turbines	machines with spinning blades that turn generators to make electricity
vacuum	an empty space that does not contain any particles of matter

INDEX